THE TALE OF A TRANSIENT LOVE

TOLD THROUGH 25 POEMS

SARA BHATIA

Copyright © Sara Bhatia
All Rights Reserved.

This book has been published with all efforts taken to make the material error-free after the consent of the author. However, the author and the publisher do not assume and hereby disclaim any liability to any party for any loss, damage, or disruption caused by errors or omissions, whether such errors or omissions result from negligence, accident, or any other cause.

While every effort has been made to avoid any mistake or omission, this publication is being sold on the condition and understanding that neither the author nor the publishers or printers would be liable in any manner to any person by reason of any mistake or omission in this publication or for any action taken or omitted to be taken or advice rendered or accepted on the basis of this work. For any defect in printing or binding the publishers will be liable only to replace the defective copy by another copy of this work then available.

To the someone I haven't met yet

Contents

Contents

Preface

Locked rooms, daydreaming episodes, and summer romances plagued with naivety - that's the pre-packaged notion of teenage years.

Adults often remark, "teenage is both a crucial and happy time of our life." Then, they'll gladly overlook the emotional complexities, and hardships teenagers face.

They assume teenagers do not possess the wisdom or the experience to pursue new challenges or meaningful relationships. To them, teenage romances are doomed.

There is no denying teenagers like us lack worldly experience. At a time when they are in a state of flux—where they debate on whether they should be expressive or enclosed, whether one should be studious or fun-loving, people waste no time saying, 'you're moody.'

But why are we set for inevitable failure? Is it because of the melodrama? Is it because teens lack emotional support and long-term goals? Is it because they are merely drawn to a relationship's novelty? Or is it just the reception of mixed reactions from parents, peers and institutions?

You were *us* in your early years, weren't you? So, what happened?

In this cascade of life where we expect and encounter hopelessness and disappointment, I chose to write this collection, not just for the teens but also for adults, to remind them what it means to love again. You may encounter bouts of longingness and pain, but I urge you to find and fall in love all over again.

To you, I beseech, throw logic out of the window. Find the intimacy you've been craving. For it may last a season, but it's not insignificant.

And when you do, try to see us in a new light.

Acknowledgements

My first debt is to my parents, who have supported me throughout the making of this book. They've always paid attention to my interests and talents and have encouraged me to keep moving forward.

Secondly, I'd like to thank my late grandma, who has played a crucial role in shaping my personality. Being an avid listener and my first best friend, she was always there for me.

My English teacher, Mr Bijit, too has played an important role. I wouldn't ever have thought about getting my poems published if he hadn't given me the idea of letting the whole world read them. I was always hesitant about having people read what I write, but when he first looked at them, he helped me reach a publishing house. And for that reason, I thank 'The Tale of You', for finding a home to this collection of mine.

Lastly, I owe a lot to *him*, whose existence I'm unsure of - the imaginary person this book is about. His thoughts have always led me to write poem after poem. I can't predict if *he* is reading this right now, but if you're out there, somewhere, you mean a lot to me.

1. Parting with the Wind

Perhaps it's the way your eyes look at mine
after I give you a long, long
hug
Or the way your fingers tangle up with mine
when you lay your head on my shoulder as we cuddle
Or the way your touch feels when you slip your hands
into my sweater
Damn, it does make me feel better
I can't get used to your absence
I can't express my love
for the 'it's complicated' relation we have
reminds me of you
after one bad day I had
Or maybe it's the way our hands knock each other
as we walk past that little garden
Maybe
it's the girl
who always makes me feel insecure?
I wish I could keep you forever
like I kept my little Mickey stuffed toy by my side
when I was little
I remember an angel whispering something into my ear

on some night
'The truth is bitter'

"Perhaps"

The angel said
"You'll leave each other
sooner or later
You'll switch your paths
be it for the worse or better"
Regardless
I need you to be here
I need you to stay
for as long as possible
Because in the end,
my hope disguised as a prayer
will come to you
like a whisper

2. Like Parallel Lines, Like Us

We'd rather be parallel lines
Although they don't meet,
ever,
they're always next to each other
They don't touch each other
or probably kiss,
but they're sittin',
staring at each other
for long
They don't seem to get tired,
because when they walk
they're staring too
But the thing about the lines
that intersect
is that once they meet
they change pathways
right and left
or
up and down
They do not stay put

on each other
like parallel lines,
like us
Parallel lines -
even if they stop walking,
they won't stop being beside
each other;
sure, they can't hug
or hold hands
but it's better than being intersecting lines
who once touch,
and then,
disband
Nor can they feel the warmth of the other one
on rough days
but at least they can stare
like the moments
when
I look at you and you're already looking
and it is more than enough to
compensate
for a hug
or a kiss
and have us alluring
I'm sure they cry
for the fact that they see each other
every day

every minute
every second
but fail to touch their little fingers
like how it's gonna be us
in the near future
when we'll crave
but will fail to touch each other

"It saddens me"

but I know that the distance cannot separate two parallel lines
because they can still stare at each other's brown eyes
or look at the soft lips
or probably hair
that they can't touch
but sure, they can see the other one
every day
every minute
every second
and not fail to have their souls meet

3. What about Leaving?

Tell me,
what would you do
if I told you about all my insecurities?
Will you still look at me
~ like I'm your Saru? ~
or will you prefer to escape?
Will you make me say:
'he ran through?'
Or would you rather say:
'Baby girl, I still love you!'
Will you run away and leave a rocky pathway
for me to walk on?
Or will you hold my hand and we'll run somewhere?
Would you look at me like I'm your Saru?
Or will you leave, as some do?

"Will you fade away like I never was a thing?"

Or would you hand me a bouquet of kisses?
and say, 'Baby girl, I still love you.'

4. You're Not Dead

Isn't it scary?

Now that you're gone

we'll never meet again.

We'll never see each other's faces

I think about you in the shower

when in the bed, even when I'm busy

I deny it when they say you're dead

You're not, right?

You're out there, just not near me

"You're there, right?"

5. Love that Flickers

No, it's something else
I can feel it gushing down my arteries
I can feel it in my bones
my tendons
Perhaps it's my love for you
like a flickering light
It flickers
here and there

"but it shall never extinguish"

6. Perhaps Loving Someone is Confusing At First

Why is it so contradictory?
The fact that some days
you're thankful for someone
while on other days, you almost wish
you guys never met
Why is it that
some days you view yourself as better
while on other days
you feel you don't deserve them?
Why do I sometimes
think of you as 'the person' in my life
while on other days
I feel I might have found
someone new
Why do I want to sob in your arms
and want you to console me?

"While on other days, I feel
you're the reason I want to sob"

Why is it that
sometimes
we behave as if we're the closest
that two people can ever be
and other times
we don't bother to talk?
I think I might have an answer
But there aren't enough lines in a notebook
to say what I need to
And now when you read this piece
You're gonna ask me whom it is about
while I sit back and justify it as mere imagination

7. Prophecy, Mine

I think we'll just
feel for each other
crave for each other's touch
love one another
and realize we ended up

"telling stories
about the other
to our spouses"

8. I Don't Exist in Your Life Anymore

She'll soon
take my place
in the game of your life
The teams will change:
a new goalkeeper
a new centre forward
a new attacker
while you'll be the lead
and I-
I will sit in the amphitheatre
waiting
for you to be done with her
Waiting for you to leave her
'cause that's what
I've always done

"waited for people"

to reply back
and to choose me

as their last resort
I'll wait
but I'll never search for a new one
for I know
you do not possess
the patience
my love requires
and you'll be in her bed
while I'll be on my couch
with your pictures in my hand
and the bracelet you once gifted
Now you'll save seats for her
whenever you reach school early
and she shall perform the same
while I-
I'll think about
how you once looked at me
with those innocent eyes
sitting on the seat next to mine
And my naïve soul
When it wakes up every morning
still longs to meet yours
like it once did
when we wrapped our arms around each other
it'll wait for you to walk past that window
and enter through the classroom door
it'll long for you to fight other people

to sit on the seat next to mine
I'll remember how you
once held me
that day I cried after
a bad day
And now you hold her
not for the fact
that she's had one too
but for the fact that
she's me in your life now

9. Words: Unsaid, Unheard

I'm short of words
to explain
what your presence
means to me.
I wish I could tell you
all that is in my head
for you

"But I do not possess
the mouth to say them
nor would you have the ears to hear"

10. 14th December 2021

Remember when we first hugged
'Have I made it up to you?' I asked
'No' you said,
as your shoulders snuggled
I hugged tighter and tighter
until I could feel your bones,
blood gushing down your arteries
and your
heart beating out of your chest
The next time we hugged
'Tighter' said I
and I realised it was a drug
too addictive to not let you go
too warm to make me cry
We exhaled in each other's arms
and at that moment, I wasn't even afraid to die
For the thing I longed for was most dearly mine
Beside the dining table
you snuggled your hands around my waist
I squeezed my hands round your neck
our heads tilted
in the arms of one another;

we perfectly fitted
I withdrew myself
you walked away
I held your waist to pull you closer
to cherish it someday
when we'd be gone from each other
We held each other tight
for the thing I most lovingly longed for was finally mine
I withdrew myself
you walked away
I held your neck and we kissed
Tired, my head dropped
your shoulder remained, and we hugged
"I love you," you exhaled
"I love you more," said I
We sat on the couch
your head dropped
and my shoulder remained
You held my fingers
I clutched your hand
My heart told me
"Make this last forever"
But the brain said "It's a drug
too addictive to not let him go
too warm to make you cry"
We hugged again, smelled one another
Time had stopped

This time
not a single word did we utter
But what if when you're gone, I don't hug anyone else?
What if I don't feel like holding anyone else's hand?
What if I don't kiss him as we do

"because they're not you?"

11. Musings at 1 AM

I'm aching here for you
writing
dreaming
thinking
about you.
Wishing you were still here
while maybe you're
in her bed.
I get flashbacks
from the time
I spent with you.
My heart is sore
from the ache you left behind.

"Perhaps you're
in your bed
dreaming
thinking
about her"

While I'm hurting
breaking

longing
just to be with you.

12. Cautionary Tale of Adulting

I wish I knew about this earlier
Now all that unknowingness kills me
The ghosts of losing, breaking, and weeping
haunt me in my sleep
I wish I knew growing up was not easy

"for I always wished to be an adult
and stay free"

Little did I know that being free was from a land far far away
Now the desires of being unchained have turned into
disillusioned dreams

13. Flashforward

I wish

God gave me

"a trailer of my life"

before my mom gave me birth

14. The Sun's my Security Blanket

The melancholy darkness hides a little world in itself -
a world contradicting euphoria.
It is a dreary realm
The sun sleeps, weeping in Memoria.
It sleeps exhausted
lets none know
for it has no one to share
its warmth with

"And yet
it wakes up bright and pleasant"

just the way you know

15. Conversation with the Stars

Do you see those stars glimmering in the night sky?
I look at them
They look at me
I see them smiling

"They sigh"

looking at the two of us
sitting together
"Shh...he's sleeping with his head rested on her shoulder."
"At last
they're together
Look at them
look how they're falling for each other."

16. ~A Boy Seeking Solace~

trying to sleep
holding his head
~partially dead~
He sowed the seeds of kindness
but depression was all he reaped
trying each side
For hours, he couldn't sleep
He tried to scream but his head was underwater
He could run away
but what he had was just a dollar
He saw them standing right there
kinda thought they might care
The day faded soon
and in the embrace of the night
it was a series of talks
that kept him alive

17. ~The Boy, Lonely like the Moon~

'Wept lonely like the moon

"while they witnessed like the stars"

He slept devastated in the sky of his bedroom
while the passersby viewed his only scars
He seemed inaudible like the Luna

"while they were maligned like the orbs"

He kept trying to fit in
with those common odds

18. ~The Boy: Lonely, Learning~

Slept with depression, bathed in anxiety
For these two stayed with him, longer than most people did
When sleeping became an escape and eating was no longer a
priority
you find yourself buried in a deep cave of anxiety

"Well, he never shared with anyone
For he was scared to be questioned
'Was scared to be lonely...."

since he seemed so hollow already
The cave seemed to bring life at a pause
and made it hard to escape all those illusionary walls
marching in depression, scared of all those confessions
But he learnt how to be strong
for all those dimensions brought with them
a new set of intentions

19. How I'll Fall Asleep on a Sleepless Night

I would be able to sleep
on a sleepless night
if only
I come under the asylum
of your voice
with my head placed
on the area
between your knees and abdomen
and your fingers
tangling up with mine
your hands slipped into my shirt
layering up my skin

"It is only then
I wouldn't need a blanket"

and we shall relive

20. When I'm With You

The part of me that got lost
somewhere in the woods
of growing up
finally comes out
searching for me

"When I'm with you
these things that have piled up
with blocks falling down
seem to cease"

and I feel okay
when I'm with you
Each teardrop
I've shed
becomes worth it
when I'm with you
Leaving behind all those people
I've left behind
becomes worth it
when I'm with you

21. Do You Still Love Me?

I had a dream
we were hanging out
Then, I got pissed and walked away
but -
you never really consoled me

"unlike how you did"

when we were in high school
and I used to be insecure
about you
whenever you told me about a new girl
or girls
I was so annoyed
and all you said was
"I assure you, I do love you"

22. Here's How I Meet You Again

23. Knife in My Heart

It was as though
someone had plunged a knife
into my heart
while it stayed there
I was tremendously pained
I struggled
For I knew if I took it out
it'd hurt even more

"So, I took it out"

24. Shadows Behind a
Smile

It's funny how people hide a gallon of mysteries behind a tint of
their smile

"things that no one knows
things that no one cares about"

Those mysteries are neither the fairy tales
nor they themselves
Those mysteries are bound to turn into loneliness
eventually
Those mysteries are nothing but
~the melancholy~

25. Love, The Rain

People view rain as a symbol of demise
when all the flowers wilt and
the clouds seem to burst
But for me, it is affection
as their warmth will arise
when all the flowers in my garden bloom
and birds seem to quench their thirst
For me

"it's the season of affection
in disguise"

Bio

Sara Bhatia is an 11th grader who likes to write poems. She's standing on a thin line, confused, whether to give up or see how much more she can take. She utilizes most of her time by studying for exams, talking to friends, binge-watching shows or listening to music. *The Tale of a Transient Love* is her debut release.